Why is it bedtime?

Written by Sally Morgan
Illustrated by Mark Ruffle

Collins

What's in this book?

Listen and say 🎧①

bed

sleep

Download the audio at www.collins.co.uk/839705

 Kitty and Toby are playing a game. Daddy says, "Kitty! Toby! It's time for bed."

Toby says, "Oh dear! We're playing."
Kitty asks, "Why is it bedtime?"

Daddy says, "You're tired."

Sleep is good. We like to sleep
at night.

In the day, you run and play.

And you learn new things at school.

At night, you are tired and you sleep.

Sleep helps your body. Sleep helps you run, play and learn.

The teacher is talking. This girl is not tired. She is listening.

This boy is tired. He is not listening.

Your body likes lots of sleep.

Finn the dog sleeps in his bed, too.

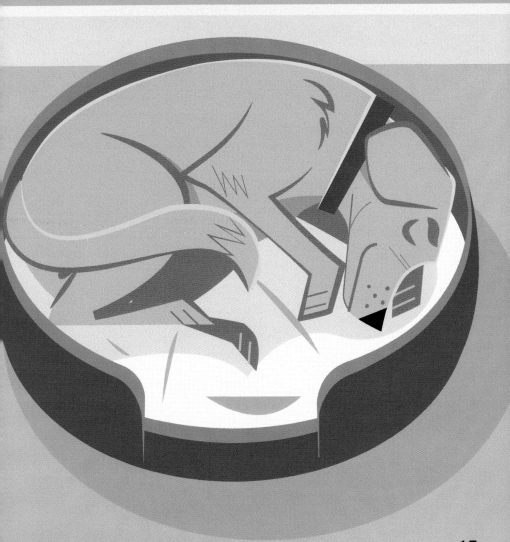

Animals sleep. This animal sleeps a lot.

It sleeps at night and it sleeps in the day.

We dream when we sleep.
What do you dream?

Animals dream too. What is Finn the dog dreaming?

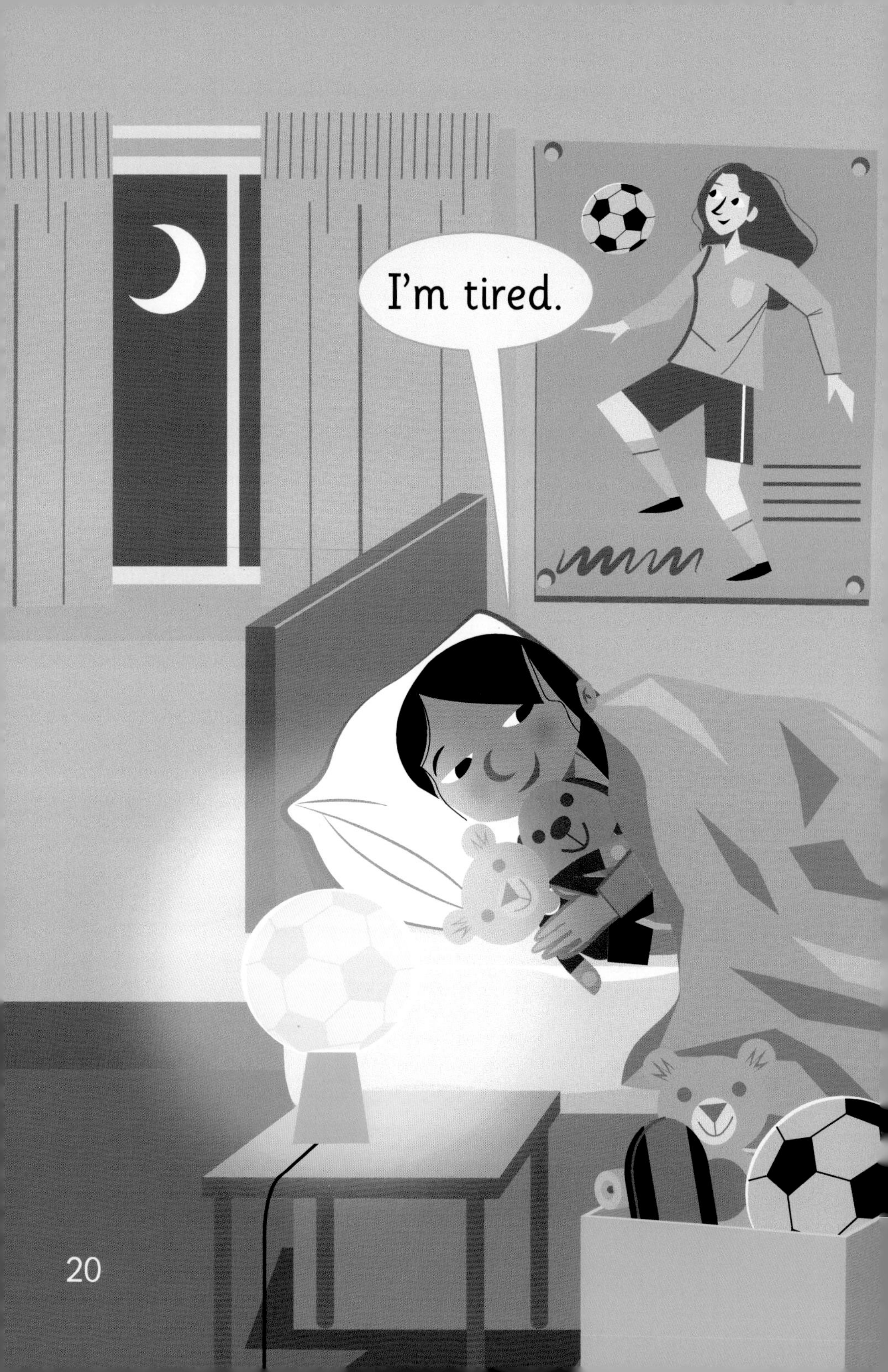
I'm tired.

Picture dictionary

Listen and repeat

dream

learn

play

run

sleep

tired

1 Look and match

It sleeps at night
and in the day.

He's sleeping.

He's tired.

This animal
is dreaming.

2 Listen and say

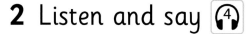

Collins

Published by Collins
An imprint of HarperCollins*Publishers*
Westerhill Road
Bishopbriggs
Glasgow
G64 2QT

HarperCollins *Publishers*
Macken House,
39/40 Mayor Street Upper,
Dublin 1
D01 C9W8
Ireland

William Collins' dream of knowledge for all began with the publication of his first book in 1819.

A self-educated mill worker, he not only enriched millions of lives, but also founded a flourishing publishing house. Today, staying true to this spirit, Collins books are packed with inspiration, innovation and practical expertise. They place you at the centre of a world of possibility and give you exactly what you need to explore it.

10 9 8 7 6 5 4 3

ISBN 978-0-00-839705-0

Collins® and COBUILD® are registered trademarks of HarperCollins*Publishers* Limited

www.collins.co.uk/elt

British Library Cataloguing in Publication Data

A catalogue record for this publication is available from the British Library.

Author: Sally Morgan
Illustrator: Mark Ruffle (Beehive)
Series editor: Rebecca Adlard
Commissioning editor: Fiona Undrill
Publishing manager: Lisa Todd
Product managers: Jennifer Hall and Caroline Green
In-house editor: Alma Puts Keren
Project manager: Emily Hooton
Editor: Barbara MacKay
Proofreaders: Natalie Murray and Michael Lamb
Cover designer: Kevin Robbins
Typesetter: 2Hoots Publishing Services Ltd
Audio produced by id audio, London
Reading guide author: Emma Wilkinson
Production controller: Rachel Weaver
Printed and bound in the UK by Pureprint

> **Download the audio for this book and a reading guide for parents and teachers at www.collins.co.uk/839705**